Practices of Blue Ribbon Catholic Schools 2001

Collected by Robert J. Kealey, Ed.D.

Edited by Janice A. Kraus

Department of Elementary Schools
National Catholic Educational Association

371.8712735
P89

Copyright 2002
National Catholic Educational Association
1077 30th St., NW, Suite 100
Washington, D.C. 20007-3852
ISBN: 1-55833-285-5

All rights reserved, including the right of reproduction in whole or part in any form. Published in the United States of America by the National Catholic Educational Association.

Table of Contents

Preface	v
Tony Boquer *School as Family*	1
Sr. M. Donna Desien *SAM: Student Assessment Meetings*	5
Jerry Ernstberger *Children's Renditions: An Evening of Art*	9
Sr. Joanne Clare Gallagher, Ms. Eileen Ryan *Musical Notes*	13
Joann Gawlik *Service Learning Program*	15
Elaine Kelly, JoAnne Risley *Partnering for Social Justice*	19
Diane Keucher *Learning & Growing Together: An Intergenerational Program at St. Charles School*	25
Stephen R. Labranche *The Behavior Log*	29
Shirley Loesch *Art Literacy Program*	33
Joan Mastell *Pizza With the Pastor*	37
Sister Theresa Maugle *Bill of Writes*	41

Barbara Migrock *Cultural Days*	45
Patricia Nugent *St. Hilary School's Enrichment Program*	47
Adele Nunez *Community Service Projects*	51
Sr. Carolyn Marie Schaffer *Transitioning Program*	57
Lois Scrivener *Effective Partnerships*	59
Sr. Mary Amata Shina, OSF, Dr. Jean Patrick, Carol Stolow *IDC: Interdisciplinary Curriculum*	63
Candace Tamposi, Gary Snyder *St. Ann's Blue Ribbon Band Program*	67
Maureen Trenary, Elaine Nikrad *Peer Ministers*	71
Elizabeth Trenkamp *A School Behavior Plan*	75
Marilyn S. Valatka, Patricia Kobyra *Reading Resources*	79
Anita J. Westerhaus *A Winning Combination: Parental Involvement and Character Counts*	83
Jackie Zufall *Student Mission Statements*	87

Preface

For almost two decades, the U. S. Department of Education has invited schools from across the country to seek the Blue Ribbon School Award. In odd numbered years elementary schools have participated and in even numbered years secondary schools have participated. NCEA has been active in encouraging its member schools to seek this award and has also offered programs to assist schools in writing their applications.

To receive this award from the U.S. Secretary of Education a school must complete a 38-page application. The test scores of the school must be significantly higher than the mean or the school must have shown continuous growth over a period of years. A committee of two reviews the application. These reviewers seek explanations of exemplary practices in the school. Each area of the application is graded. If only good grades are given to parts of the application, the school will not be considered for the award. The grades are tallied and a decision is made to send a site visitor to the school or not to have the school site visited. If the application is deemed not worthy of a site visit, the school is eliminated from the competition. A person visits the school and completes a report of what was observed and how well the actuality is presented in the application. A new team of reviewers then examines the original application and the site visitor's report. A recommendation is then made to the Secretary to grant the school Blue Ribbon status.

NCEA is proud of the large number of Catholic schools that have received this award. The Department of Elementary Schools Executive

Practices of Blue Ribbon Catholic Schools, 2001

Committee (DESEC) believes that the practices of these schools should be shared with the entire Catholic school community. Therefore, this year each of the schools receiving the award was requested to write a short article on one of the programs in the school that the principal believed to be exemplary. One of the main functions of NCEA is to share good ideas among its members.

    The NCEA Department of Elementary schools presents this work to the membership in the hope that it will encourage its members to adapt some of these practices to their schools and also to consider applying for the Blue Ribbon Schools Award in the future.

    The NCEA Department of Elementary Schools expresses its gratitude to the principals for taking the time to tell their stories so others can benefit from it. The Catholic schools of the nation are a community and a high expression of this community is the willingness to share with others. The department expresses its gratitude to Janice Kraus, its editorial assistant, who edited the materials and saw the project from its inception to its conclusion. Beatriz Ruiz of the NCEA Communications Department designed the cover and pages.

Feast of St. Katherine Drexel 2002
Department of Elementary Schools
National Catholic Educational Association

Janet P. Murray, M.A.   Robert J. Kealey, Ed.D.
President   *Executive Director*

School as Family

Tony Boquer
Principal
Holy Family Catholic Academy
Honolulu HI

Each day as students and parents arrive at Holy Family Catholic Academy, there are signs of a safe and caring environment where students feel accepted as part of the school family. Teachers open the school at 6:30 a.m. for "Before School Care" to welcome the students of working parents. A staff member opens car doors and greets families. Teachers supervise the children on the front playground where they gather for morning assembly. At 7:45 a.m., all students line up by grade level to say morning prayers and the Pledge of Allegiance. Upcoming events of the day are announced as well as special student acknowledgements. Students are praised for various accomplishments, such as reading, spelling and geography bees, team sports, music and band awards. The cheerleaders and band perform a short pep rally for special occasions. Morning assembly ends with the student body singing either a patriotic song, such as the National Anthem, or our school alma mater. By unifying in prayer and song, children not only see that they are members of a large family, but they also feel the spirit of "Hawaiian Ohana" (family).

Our emphasis is to create a warm, nurturing, supportive environment for our students. As students walk to their classrooms, they pass posters, signs, banners, and bulletin boards reflecting the monthly character trait and religious themes. The character traits are based on biblical building blocks that reflect and complement many of our monthly religious themes. Throughout the day, students are challenged and reminded to reflect upon their own characters and Christian values as they travel in the hallways.

As Christian educators, we provide opportunities to interact and build relationships with our students in order to help them grow academically and mature as Christian with a growing faith. Throughout the day, students know that they can speak to our principal, the dean of discipline, the religion teachers, or chat with Father McNeely, our pastor, for guidance. Our school provides numerous opportunities for students to interact with teachers and other adults through the many extracurricular activities, fund-raisers, and service projects. On a daily basis, individual students are treated specially. In the lower grades, each child is recognized during "Student of the Week." Students can be seen visiting Mr. Boquer, the principal, in his office to have their awards signed or to boast about their accomplishments. At the end of every month, all children with birthdays in that particular month are invited to the cafeteria for a special ice cream treat.

Students connect to other students within the school environment through peer interaction provided by cooperative learning experiences. This instills in each student a sense of identity and responsibility, and with these comes the realization that success depends on every group member. The student-led groups cooperatively communicate, analyze, and reflect on the exercise at hand in order to complete authentic tasks. They learn to listen, to evaluate, and to formulate their own sense of understanding and to value the opinions of others.

In the 1996-1997 school year, Miracy Agraan, on of our third-grade children, was diagnosed with leukemia. Miracy battled leukemia until November 1999, when she was in sixth grade. During the three years Miracy was in and out of the hospital, our school name "Holy Family" was put to the test. Our school became a true family ... caring, loving, and praying for Miracy and her family. Students and teachers visited Miracy not only in the hospital, but also at home. Students wrote and called with school information and news that would brighten her day. Mementos, pictures, and treasures were given to Miracy to lift her spirits. When Miracy returned after losing her hair, many of her classmates wore hats as she did, making her feel comfortable. During recess time, Miracy was never alone. Students sat and played quiet games in the shade with her. We prayed for Miracy during morning assemblies, lunchtime rosary groups, and with our school parents. Academic and curriculum adjustments were made to help her during periods when she was weak. When Miracy went to be with the Lord in November, 1999, the school band fulfilled her final request by playing her favorite song at her funeral.

SAM: Student Assessment Meetings

Sr. M. Donna Desien
Corpus Christi School
Wilmington, DE

SAM is a common "in school" word at Corpus Christi School in Wilmington, DE. This acronym stands for "Student Assessment Meetings" which underpins much of the teachers' work in helping the most needy students. The meetings are held quarterly, prior to report card writing and distribution. Present at these meetings are the principal, counselor, and teachers of the students who have surfaced as having academic, behavioral or social needs preventing them from reaching their full potential. Prior to the actual meeting, groundwork has occurred in the classroom. All teachers in kindergarten through grade eight assess student performance by informal observations, teacher made tests, as well as, text reviews and tests. In March of each year the students take standardized tests. This tool, along with the above-mentioned assessments, help to identify students needing early intervention and guidance, as well as pointing the way for whatever accommodations need to be made.

Since this program has been in existence for nearly fourteen years, and our teacher turnover is minimal, we feel that the students' needs are met at very early ages thus preventing failure in the upper elementary and in the middle school. Of course, as we all know, a new series of challenges will often present themselves at the upper levels.

Several of our teachers responded to the question, "How has SAM assisted you in trying to better meet the needs of your students?" Rosemary Deery, a fifth-grade teacher, noted "...that a team approach which considers all aspects of the student's development is always more enlightening and successful simply because it heightens an awareness of a student's needs and provides diverse input and expertise. A fuller picture can be gained when the student's past history, habits, academic record, social standing, and parent involvement are considered when trying to remediate a current problem. When a plan of action is formulated by all who are involved with a student, there is agreement and consistency in the follow-up. Having the counselor and administration present ensures that nothing falls between the slats and that everything is considered."

Our middle school faculty also affirms the help received. Donna Slivinski, eighth-grade math teacher, felt that the part of SAM which helps her most is "... meeting with the other middle school teachers to receive a current update on the student's progress in each of his/her classes. This keeps the student's changing needs ever in my mind." Michele Alexander, a seventh-grade teacher, felt that "Input from the principal and school counselor gave me an historical perspective of the student's educational experience and aided in successfully helping me to better understand various learning styles." Another middle school teacher, Terry Hoban, felt that "... having the opportunity to, share concerns in confidence with our SAM team, enables us to recognize needs early and make timely recommendations."

Recognition of the SAM team as a confidential group of professionals who share ideas and strategies, thus enabling targeted children to learn/grow in all areas, was mentioned by the kindergarten teachers. They also noted that the school counselor was involved in all stages of problem solving including assessment, observation, parent conferences, record keeping and even outside professional assessment by psychologists/physicians.

Jane Unsay, a third-grade teacher, remarked that "... the part of SAM which I felt had been the most successful for me was that the scheduled meetings help keep me aware of the objectives I hope to accomplish, because the meetings provide time for consistent updating and it was in this consistency that I can keep abreast of my students' needs." Rosemary Deery, quoted earlier, said," When I have gone back and followed up with my "to do list" for each student, I know exactly what I need to say to parents and/or students to make things happen. When parents are cooperative, I have had tremendous results from the SAM recommendations and discussions."

During the past two years, extensions of the program have been made to include input from all special areas namely: art, computer, physical education and Spanish. A special form is sent to these teachers two weeks prior to the SAM team meeting. Frequently a child's performance in these areas can give valuable insight to the team. Mary Ann Harry, the art teacher for all of our students, commented, "... input is valuable since seeing students from many viewpoints helps us to know and understand the scope of the total child."

In our Blue Ribbon Report, we enumerated some data for the previous academic year which showed the number of students who moved into groups with more challenging course work as well as some students who needed more intense help. We look carefully at the individual student to assess further direction based on past performance and present need. In some cases, it is necessary to recommend outside professional assistance to fully accommodate individual needs.

As Rosemary Deery so aptly stated, "The recommendations that are made are usually clear 'to do's' which have helped me to manage the situation. Having SAM three times a year and documenting the findings ensures that there is timely follow-up to something that could easily get dropped. If problems resurface down the road, then there is a record of how it was handled. Special notation should be made that this is an excellent time for all who work with a student to review testing, discuss findings, and then put into action the recommendations. These meetings assure that this is accomplished."

To the credit of the teachers, along with the principal and counselor, early detection and successful intervention are the hallmarks of our SAM program which has helped to reduce academic and social failure at Corpus Christi School, a two time Blue Ribbon recipient.

Children's Renditions: An Evening of Art

Jerry Ernstberger
Principal
Holy Family School
New Albany, IN

Holy Family School has many wonderful traditions and programs, and the school enjoys tremendous support from our parents and parish community. Our parent group, the Holy Family Home and School Association (HSA), is a vibrant organization which serves the school through many special activities which include fellowship activities, fund raising, classroom support, and community service. One of our parent-led programs has blossomed into a wonderful community project that enhances our community and provides needed services for students and their families.

One major goal of the HSA is to support the budget to offset the tuition costs for school families. For the past five years, HSA has sponsored a gala dinner auction to raise funds and friends for the school. Like many school fundraising events, this evening brings together school supporters and parishioners who enjoy a wonderful catered dinner in our gymnasium and bid on silent and live auction items.

Each year is marked by a special theme that pervades the auction atmosphere and decor. The children and parents alike enjoy the magical transformation of the gym into a far-off place and time. Past auction themes have included *A Night at the Oscars, Under the Big Top, South of the Border,* and *Tropical Paradise.* This year our theme is *Children's Renditions: an Evening of Art.*

Each year students participate in the auction, especially through their class art projects. Bid items include wonderful student artworks, such as a photo quilt of the eighth grade class, handmade chess sets by seventh graders, painted patio furniture and children's furniture, and self-portrait prints by kindergartners. Students also participate in an auction program cover contest, in which they compete for prizes and to have their drawing be selected as cover for the auction program. Last year, the entire student body participated in the cover contest. While the students do not attend the dinner gala, our "family fun night" gives them an opportunity to enjoy the festive atmosphere of the auction with games, face painting, musical entertainment and food.

This year our theme is *Children's Renditions,* a very special project is being developed by our creative parents and faculty. Two of our parents are chairing the project and providing the classroom teachers with extensive artistic support. Students have begun creating giant art works imitating the works of known contemporary artists. Each class has selected an artist to study and imitate. Seventh graders recently splashed, sprinkled and flecked large six feet by fifteen feet canvases in the style of Jackson Pollock. These canvases will be hung from the gym ceiling as decorations for the auction event. Other classes are creating large scale works by artists such as Henri Matisse's *Icarus,* Jasper Johns' *Three Flags,* Wassily Kandinsky's *Trente 1937,* and Andy Warhol's *Marilyn.* Other featured artists include Pablo Picasso, Joan Miro and Salvador Dali. Students will draw, paint, or cut and paste their own rendition on two-feet square foam boards. These will be pieced together creating a larger work by the entire class. These giant artworks will provide the backdrop for the entire gymnasium. Hanging Alexander Calder sculptures designed and crafted by eighth graders will dangle over the dinner tables as centerpieces.

Students are learning more about these famous artists and their contributions to the art world. They learn about contemporary art themes and styles. In addition, they create a personalized rendition of their own for the gymnasium decor. Students will enjoy seeing their works hanging in our "school gallery."

One of the truly remarkable elements of the art project is the sense of wonder and discovery that students find in studying contemporary art. The non-traditional forms, colors and shapes enable students to develop their own creative talents. As stated by one of our parents, "I think this is a great theme to make the analogy of our children as works of art unfolding ... not yet complete ... where the color and strokes of each day make every child unique and beautiful. Each child is a masterpiece to be appreciated. pondered over and valued as priceless."

Musical Notes

Sister Joanne Clare Gallagher
Principal

Ms. Eileen Ryan
Our Lady Queen of Angels School
Newport Beach, CA

The faculty and staff of Our Lady Queen of Angels School believes that the partnership between God, students, and family is one of the most important reasons parents enroll their students at the school. Religious instruction is a part of the daily academic life, whether in a dedicated religion class, attendance of services with clergy, or as an integral component of all instruction. This has been the key our school's success in developing moral consciousness in our youth and their commitment to become responsible citizens. Our Lady Queen of Angels students are active participants in church activities, either by singing in the choir, serving as altar servers, participating in the Catholic Youth Organization, participating in prison ministry. helping Habitat for Humanity, or helping feed homeless people, and serving numerous other charitable organizations that minister to our community.

Our Lady Queen of Angels Children's Choir, "Musical Notes," is a popular school organization that is well recognized in the community. The choir complements the religious programs at the school and provides superior musical training for students. Musical Notes furthers education by teaching spiritual songs and life-long skills such as singing techniques, music reading, and rhythm instrument playing. Students in grades five through eight also have the unique opportunity to receive special training in handbell performance. Not only does the choir perform for weekly mass, it is also the centerpiece for the parish and school community at Christmas, First Communion and other events. The program's finale includes a spring musical combining musical performance, acting and artistic design. Over 60% of the student population participates in this co-curricular activity during their years at Our Lady Queen of Angels. This program continually receives high marks from students, teachers, parents and the community.

Students have an opportunity to develop their musical potential and increase their self-esteem through achievements that result from working together. Musical Notes also provides a unique and effective way to further religious instruction through song and discussions designed to deepen spiritual awareness and influence the formation of values. It is an important element to the school and church outreach program by bringing together the parish and school communities through music. Additionally, Musical Notes is one of several co-curricular activities designed to bring students of different grades together. Musical Notes is considered one of several important programs that contribute to the school's success and continues the tradition of the Sisters of St. Joseph of Carondelet by embracing Catholic values in all aspects of instruction to prepare students to become responsible members of society.

Service Learning Program

Joann Gawlik
Principal
Holy Spirit Catholic School
San Antonio, TX

Holy Spirit Catholic School's philosophy holds that the students are given the opportunity to develop their spiritual, moral, and intellectual foundations, enabling them to realize their full potential for a lifetime of commitment and service. Holy Spirit is held up as a model school because of its innovative ideas in curriculum development and alignment, the Honor and Resource programs, academic competitions at the local, state, and national levels, and commitment to service.

Holy Spirit Catholic School has as its primary goal the continued formation of the Christian person. This process has as its purpose the ongoing education and development of every dimension of every student, enabling each one to attain their highest possible level of growth. Teachers, students, and their families, each one according to their role and with the support of the parish, are called to proclaim the Gospel message, to unite in worship, and to respond to the needs of the community through fellowship. The school community must promote social justice and serve all people through the sharing of its spiritual gifts and temporal goods.

The Service Program, implemented through a Service Learning Model, is a key component in fulfilling the school's philosophy and mission. Monthly service projects, which focus on local, national, or worldwide needs, involve the students in bringing about a positive change for others. School-wide class discussions and projects, faculty and parent involvement, and community participation help to prepare students for life in a complex and diverse society. Through this active participation in the practices of community service, faith and citizenship are brought together to help students put into practice the social teachings of the Catholic Church.

The student body demonstrates its commitment to the local, national, and world communities through numerous service projects, including the San Antonio Mission Ministries (Socks for SAMM project), Native American Missions (Pennies for People campaign) and African Missions (Middle School Cake Raffle proceeds). In addition to the planned monthly school-wide service projects, Holy Spirit Church and school have a history of responding to opportunities or crises as they arrive. The school and parish collected $55,000 for a school family to begin a yearlong mission at a Mexican orphanage beginning July 2000. The school community also responded by donating money, clothes, prayer, and manpower to help Holy Spirit's coach and fellow citizens who lost everything in the devastating floods in San Antonio and Del Rio.

With an outpouring of emotional and spiritual support, Holy Spirit served as a gathering place for blood drives, prayer vigils, and subsequent memorial services after a tragic four-person fatal accident at Antonian College Prep, with which our Holy Spirit community has close ties. Holy Spirit continues to host blood drives in their honor. The school community, especially the students, again pulled together to offer prayers and emotional support and raise money after the sudden death of one of our beloved custodians, whose wife also works forth parish. The students and PTC sold Frito pies during lunch and donated all the money to the family. Many students gave their allowances in addition to purchasing lunch.

Commitment to service is also evident in our parent population. As often cited by visiting families, part of what makes Holy Spirit so special is the incredible army of devoted volunteers who make the school buzz with a great cooperative spirit. Through our "Parents as Partners" program, each single parent family contributes a minimum of ten service hours annually, while two parent families donate twenty hours. Parents, parishioners, the pastor, staff, and alumni lend their time and talent daily from the lunchroom, to the classroom, to the library. Staff and parents are visible as volunteers in the liturgies, and classrooms, as coaches, and during service projects. More than 7,000 hours of community service were recorded last year by the school's parents and teachers. The program has a 96% participation rate and has been a model for other local schools.

Having these excellent adult role models influences even the youngest Holy Spirit students. They see service and responsibility in action and discover how helping one another can build a productive community. As a result, Holy Spirit has earned a longstanding reputation for excellent, civic-minded students, both in and out of the classroom. Students participate in school liturgies, after-school activities, and in community service projects as ambassadors of the school. Middle school students serve as tour guides and peer tutors. In addition, students are involved in Junior Achievement, DARE, St. Vincent de Paul Society, Career Day, Habitat for Humanity, CYO, National Junior Honor Society, Student Council and city recycling programs. Every middle school student is expected to contribute twenty hours of community service annually to the school, their families, their city, and other countries in need. Their efforts in volunteerism help prepare them to be socially concerned and responsible adults.

Many any of the school's alumni move on to serve as leaders in their high schools, colleges and universities, and in the community. Their accomplishments are highlighted in Holy Spirit's monthly newsletters. In addition, these former students even return to Holy Spirit to "give something back" by volunteering as coaches, speakers and substitute teachers. Many younger alumni volunteer service hours to complete their high school or religious education requirements.

Service projects offer multiple opportunities to be active in real-life problem-solving experiences. School activities and service projects connect math application skills to real world situations. Students count and sort canned goods for the St. Vincent de Paul Society, group and classify (according to size and color) bears and other stuffed animals donated to the San Antonio Police Department's Kids in Crisis, and tabulate money collected for missions in Mexico. Students use measurement skills, geometry, and spatial concepts when they design sets for the eighth grade play. Mental math, estimation, money skills, and calculators are used in student fundraising activities. The annual Archdiocesan Spirit Day engages each class at Holy Spirit in friendly competition, raising money for the school's capital improvement projects. Students learn counting and graphing skills as they watch the colorful donation charts change daily.

Supported by the administration, staff, parents, parish and community, these school-wide and community initiatives help develop a Catholic identity rooted in the social teachings of our Church. Students can take an active part in identifying and meeting the needs of others while developing future leadership roles in the Church and the community.

Partnering for Social Justice

Elaine Kelly
Director of Religious Education

JoAnne Risley
Director of Curriculum
Waldron Mercy Academy
Merion Station, PA

> *Connect the rich to the poor, the healthy to the sick, the educated and skilled to the uninstructed, the influential to those of no consequence, the powerful to the weak to do the work of God on earth."* This is the legacy of Sister Catherine McAuley, foundress of the Sisters of Mercy.

Empowered by gospel values and the spirit of mercy, the Waldron Mercy Academy community endeavors to rise to the challenge of Catherine McAuley. Waldron Mercy Academy has a long-standing history of reaching out to the poor in the neighboring communities to provide basic resources such as food, clothing, and other necessities while offering signs of caring such as cards, prayers, and gift-giving. For many years outreach activities included annual peanut butter and jelly collections, Thanksgiving food baskets, coat drives, Christmas gifts, and almsgiving from an annual Lenten walk-a-thon. A monthly dessert day evolved into a bagged lunch collection aptly named H.O.P.E. (Help Other People Eat). But something was missing. Although we were collecting very useful things, we were giving them to nameless, faceless people ... the poor, the needy, the hungry, the homeless. A deeper connection was needed. Who were these people? How did they come to these circumstances?

To create a meaningful connection, we restructured our program to develop a closer relationship with our outreach ministries. Twelve years ago we developed a successful relationship with the people of St. Columba Shelter, a residence for homeless men. Our school community of parents, teachers, and students began to cook and serve bi-monthly dinners for the residents. Our connection had such a positive effect on all who became involved there that we decided to search for additional avenues of service, not only to develop our students' sense of civic responsibility, but also to put their faith into action. To facilitate this effort we linked each grade to a different social service agency or school. These included a home for the aged, shelters for formerly homeless men, women, and children, a daycare center for physically and mentally challenged adults, a home for AIDS patients, an inner city public school in an impoverished neighborhood, and a classroom of severely challenged children in a Philadelphia public school. In addition, faculty and staff have their own outreach ministry to the Catholic Worker House of Grace and Women of Change, a shelter for formerly homeless women. All members of our community are invited to share their time and talent to make a difference and to expand our program with their ideas and input.

Parents volunteer to serve as liaisons between the outreach ministry and each grade. They contact the agency to create a wish list and coordinate the efforts of the teachers, parents, and students of the particular grade to provide the requested necessities. A representative from each service agency or school comes to Waldron Mercy Academy to speak to individual grades and may show slides or a video to help them understand the plight of the people with whom they will be partnered for that school year. The children ask questions and are invited to share their feelings in discussions to promote a deeper understanding of those they will be helping. Where feasible and appropriate, our students visit their outreach partners in the residences or schools. In addition to bringing needed items, casseroles, and holiday treats and gifts, our students talk with their partners, sing for them, read to them, and pray with them. Many of our outreach partners have been invited to shows, picnics, and other special events at Waldron Mercy Academy. Classes partnering with physically and mentally challenged children take them on shopping trips to the mall or out to lunch. Inner city children are invited to spend a day with their partners on our campus.

In addition to the ministries already mentioned, a new venture for us this year is a connection with the missions of the Sisters of Mercy in Peru. Our fifth-graders are currently raising funds to buy an additional sewing machine for the Peruvian women who make clothing to sell as a means of income. Additional funds raised by the class will be used for much needed vitamins and antibiotics. This is one small step toward raising consciousness and developing a sense of responsibility for our brothers and sisters worldwide.

"If you want peace, work for justice." These words of Pope Paul VI became our driving thought: when a conversion of attitude and stereotypes takes place, the chance of systemic change occurring is enhanced. We knew we needed to move the outreach program from isolated activities of service to meaningful integration into the curriculum. Language arts teachers guide their classes in writing prayers and letters and help them use their computer skills to make holiday cards and invitations for their outreach ministry. Math teachers incorporate measuring and direction skills into baking bread for the shelters. Social studies teachers use current events magazines, daily newspapers, and Channel One to spark discussions. Journal writing, reflections, and idea-sharing take place around poverty, homelessness, hunger, rejection by society, and other forms of injustice to assist our students in developing a global perspective and a social conscience.

A social justice unit was recently designed by one of our upper grade teachers to encourage activism and show our students how to address the problems of homelessness, discrimination, and poverty on a broader level. Advocacy is an area of service learning that we are developing and plan to expand. For many years our school community has celebrated Peace and Justice Day. This year, in addition to a school-wide community gathering, which includes a prayer service, songs, and readings of our students' reflections and poetry about peace and justice, the upper grades will have an assembly on Alfred Nobel and the Nobel Peace Prizewinners. Reflecting on the actions of these models for peace could challenge our students to create a vision and to set goals for working toward a more just society and a more peaceful society.

Our students get to know that the people to whom we minister are ordinary people with names, desires, gifts, talents, a past, a present, and a future. The children see first-hand that what they do directly impacts these individual lives and makes a difference. They develop a sense of compassion and caring which evolves into a value system that includes a responsibility to those less fortunate. Through our compassionate care, the recipients know that others are concerned for them and their well being. Their gift to us is a better understanding of the value of relationships over the material things of this world. Members of the Waldron Mercy Academy community gain an appreciation for the life experiences of others and the hardships that they endure. In addition to helping our students build character and develop a sense of civic responsibility, our community outreach program fulfills our mission of promoting gospel values, understanding and appreciating diversity, and helps our students to become agents of change for social justice.

People outside our community have expressed amazement that elementary school children could be involved in something so ambitious. On the contrary, we believe that we are simply taking small steps, trying to walk in the way Jesus showed us, seeking to include all people in our circle of love, giving each person the respect and dignity owed them as a child of God.

In closing we ask you to reflect on the words of Edward Everett Hale:

I am only one,
But still I am one.
I cannot do everything,
But still I can do something.

*And because I cannot do everything,
I will not refuse to do the something
That I can do.*

…and in so doing, we then make a living response to the question posed to Micah, the prophet, "What does the Lord require of you? To do justice, and love kindness, and walk humbly with our God."

Learning and Growing Together: An Intergenerational Program at St. Charles School

Diane Keucher
Development Director
St. Charles Borromeo School
Bloomington, IN

Nowhere is it more evident that we are all life-long teachers and learners than when elders and elementary students come together for *Learning and Growing Together,* an intergenerational program at St. Charles Borromeo School in Bloomington, Indiana. Now in its seventh year, Mickey Lentz, Executive Director of Catholic Education for the Archdiocese of Indianapolis, has described the program as "the best kept secret in the nation."

Learning and Growing Together began as a three-way partnership between St. Charles School, the Indiana University Center on Aging and Aged, and participating elders. It had been a dream of Dr. Susan

Eklund, Director of the Center on Aging and Aged, to pilot a program that would bring young and old together to learn from one another and to create a greater sense of community, understanding, and shared values. Citing concerns and potential benefits for participants on both ends of the age spectrum, she wrote, "When I was a child I spent a lot of time with my grandparents and was greatly enriched by the experience. Today grandparents often live far away from their grandchildren, sometimes are separated from them through divorce. Many children have little direct contact with older adults. Most community settings are age-segregated, with schools for children and senior centers for elders. Some elders experience a sense of isolation and loss of purpose after retirement. Becoming important in the lives of children can provide connection and a renewed purpose." Dr. Eklund shared her dream with colleague Catherine Siffin, herself a graduate of St. Charles who had maintained close ties to the school through the years when her daughter and then her granddaughter were St. Charles students. Ms. Siffin thought St. Charles would be the ideal site for a pilot program. The wheels were set in motion when Dr. Eklund and Ms. Siffin presented a detailed proposal to school principal Virginia Suttner who immediately saw the benefits of the program for everyone involved.

So in the spring of 1996 eighteen elders went back to school at St. Charles. Many of them were recruited from existing groups in the parish community, including a retirees' club and a Bible study group. Topics for the intergenerational classes were chosen by three teachers, who volunteered to enrich regular curricular areas with elder participants. A second grade teacher surprised everyone by wanting to include a unit on World War II, adamant in the belief that her students were not too young to be engaged by the topic. In its first year, the World War II elder presenters included a weather outlook person who served in Greenland for seventeen months, the wife of the first service person to receive both the Congressional Medal of Honor and the Distinguished Service Cross, and an Army tank driver who had served in General Patton's division at the Battle of the Bulge. The course continues to attract others: an army pilot from the Asian theater of war, a female member of the Marine Corps, and a German war bride who grew up in Nazi Germany. A teacher at St. Charles grew up in London during its nighttime bombings and comes to share her stories with the students. Word about the course has spread; the effect is that World War II veterans often approach the teacher and offer to be elder volunteers.

Today, both of our second grade and fourth grade classes participate annually in the intergenerational program which spans a period of four to five weeks during the spring semester. We have found that unless both classes at a grade level are participating, the students in the non-participating class feel excluded and parents often seek placement for their child in the class with the intergenerational program. In each classroom two to four children are assigned to an elder. Before they ever meet one another, elders and students get acquainted through an exchange of pen-pal letters. Then the exciting day arrives when they meet each other face-to-face. Time set aside for getting-to-know-you activities is a part of every elder visit to the classrooms, allowing the students and elders to establish relationships with each other that continue to grow through the course of the program.

Students in one second grade class continue with the World War II unit. The other second grade class focuses on *Once Upon a Time*, a unit that gives elders and students the opportunity to share and compare childhood activities then and now. Both fourth grades participate in *Songfest* which is coordinated by one of the school's music teachers. True to its design, *Songfest* provides a great deal of interaction between the participants both in the classroom and when they move to the music room to practice together. Songs used are selected from surveys that elders and students complete prior to the classes. Traditional favorites include "You Are My Sunshine," "Sentimental Journey," and "Take Me Out To The Ball Game." The program culminates with a pitch-in dinner and performance for friends and families.

Over the years a model program has been developed that brings the generations together, dispels preconceptions, fosters mutual respect, and builds loving, enduring relationships. The Center on Aging and Aged has used the St. Charles model for many conference presentations, but perhaps the best assessment of the program and the relationships it fosters is given in a poem written by one class to its elders:

We like so many things about you.
We like your gentle eyes,
And how your face lights up
When you catch sight of us.

The way you listen well
To what we say,
As if our thoughts and feelings
Were the most important thing
In all the world.

Did you know that in your face
We see
Enthusiasm and serenity?
Wisdom and innocence?

And if your hair is curly, white —
Or even if you've not much hair at all —
We like that, too.

So thank you for your friendship,
For sharing your ideas
About the life you've lived;
For spoiling us,
And being on our side;

For helping us understand
That we are all connected,
All on the same journey,
All children of God.

The Behavior Log

Stephen R. Labranche
Principal
St. Francis Xavier School
Metairie, LA

Though well-intentioned and concerned about the students in our Catholic school, teachers find it almost impossible to remember every student's behavior which negatively impacts the learning process for all students. Some behaviors (e.g., "forgetting" books, no homework, etc.) are not really disciplinary in nature but rather may be considered bad habits or lack of concern by the student or parents and, while not effecting a whole class or school, are nonetheless detrimental to a student's learning, grades, and social development and acceptance.

Unlike self-contained classrooms in which the teacher is with the same students for the majority of the day and can more easily remember disruptive or unacceptable behaviors, teachers in the middle school setting only see students for one period each day and have no idea what a student may be doing in other classrooms. How then could all the teachers not only learn and remember what students are doing in other classes but also work together and with the principal to help a student change bad habits and unacceptable behaviors? The Behavior Log was developed to delineate and document those behaviors which needed to change.

Each homeroom teacher was provided a three-ring binder large enough to hold a pre-printed "behavior card" for each student in that class. On the top of the card were spaces for the student's name, homeroom, parents' home and work telephone numbers. Below double horizontal lines are vertical columns which are labeled with the date, time, offense, consequence, and remarks. The binder is labeled with the home-room name and went with the class as it moved around school throughout the day, i.e., P.E., French, Music, Computer, or, in the case of middle school, to the seven classes per day held in each homeroom.

Whenever a student failed to comply with one of the rules, regulations, or academic requirements that were listed in the school handbook, the student was written up in "the BOOK," as the students call it. When a student received three entries, a thirty-minute retention notice was issued to the student for the following school day which had to be taken home and signed by a parent. If a student received three entries on the same day, the student was sent to the school office to call a parent and see the principal.

When a student received and served three retentions, the parents were either called or called in by the principal to discuss their child's behavior. This was the result of a student having been logged in "the Book" nine times. In the lower school, children are given at least two verbal warnings before being entered in the log. This practice is patterned after "Assertive Discipline." The rules are clearly stated and enforced. The offenses and consequences are consistently logged. The students and parents are made aware of patterns of behavior that should be changed for the total well-being of the child.

In the case of middle school, for example, a student who did not have homework for first period would be given a "zero" or lose points in homework. The second-period teacher would have done the same under normal circumstances because he did not know that the student had not had homework in first period. With the "log," a flag goes up to the teacher who writes the second entry. And, whether the third entry is on the same day or the day after, a pattern is being developed and the teachers are very much aware of a lack of seriousness on the part of the student. This results in a parent/student/principal conference, which might also include the teacher(s). No student likes having his/

her parent(s) learn that (s)he has been playing the game of telling parents one tale and the school another.

This program does require a cohesive and concerted effort on the part of the faculty and administration. Teachers also spend valuable class time entering offenses in the book. At the beginning of each year, however, the children quickly learn that their antics and habits are not being overlooked and that too many visits to the principal with their parents might mean having to leave this school, which they truly love, and in which they are truly loved.

This is the fourth year of utilizing the behavior log. It has truly saved many students AND parents, who in some cases do not know what acceptable behaviors are, or how to deal with them if they do know, or have never been made aware of the absolute need for every one of us to follow the message of Jesus.

Art Literacy Program

Shirley Loesch
Principal
Our Lady of Lourdes School
Vancouver, WA

Our Lady of Lourdes School is committed to offer a full, well-rounded curriculum. Oftentimes, due to budget restraints, many schools are prohibited from offering programs beyond the core curriculum. While budget limitations are a fact of life at our school, a little creativity and a strong commitment to the arts has served as the impetus to develop an Art Literacy program for our students.

Our Art Literacy program offers our students a remarkable opportunity to explore the visual arts. It is a multi-sensory experience covering a wide variety of art media and styles, across time and cultural boundaries, from cave drawings to those created with contemporary technological tools. Our Art Literacy program is staffed entirely by volunteers, with limited budget funds available for materials and supplies.

Each year in the spring, the Art Literacy team meets to plan its curriculum for the coming school year. Volunteers specialize in each grade level (primary, intermediate and middle school) and coordinate and collaborate with respective teachers to incorporate art lessons into the class curriculum and schedule. Ideas and inspiration for Art Literacy lessons are derived from a variety of sources. The Art Literacy team reviews the upcoming exhibition schedule for the Portland Art Museum and looks at ways to incorporate their lessons with the museum's exhibits. They also look for ways to incorporate the theme of the school's annual auction in the art lessons. For example, a Mardi Gras theme inspires a lesson on the history and creation of masks. Overall, the Art Literacy team is working to create a diverse mix of artists and art forms. The Art Literacy team obtains demonstration art for each lesson (borrowing materials from the local libraries or purchasing materials if necessary), and determines and purchases necessary materials for hands-on projects created by the students.

Age-appropriate lessons are developed by the Art Literacy team and presented to the students on a monthly basis. Lessons, presented by Art Literacy volunteers, focus on a particular artist or cultural art form, including examples of the work, and often complimented by samples of music from the artist's era or culture. Each lesson culminates with a hands-on project in which students create a work of art that emulates the style of the artist they have just studied. Projects have included various styles of painting, sculpture, quilting, and storybook illustration, to name just a few. Every student has the opportunity to participate and receive positive feedback and encouragement for their creative expression. Students also have the opportunity to select their favorite samples and take pride in displaying their work at an annual Art Fair in the spring.

The Art Literacy at Our Lady of Lourdes School also offers natural crossover connections to the regular classroom curriculum. Art Literacy projects have featured the styles of children's book illustrators well known to primary age students. The middle school's study of Russian history was enriched with a study of religious icons, which, in turn, inspired a field trip to a Russian Orthodox church. To further enhance the study of Russian history and art, the Art Literacy team arranged an all-school trip to the Stroganoff Exhibit at the Portland Art Museum. A recent architecture project was coupled with the study of Washington history and the prominent architecture of Mother Joseph in the Vancouver/Portland area. A visit from Mother Joseph herself, in the person of an assembly presenter, further enriched this experience for the entire student body.

The Art Literacy program at Our Lady of Lourdes School has been an overwhelming success with students, teachers, and parents. We are proud that we have been able to design an Art Literacy program that provides valuable education in the visual arts, enables valued input from our parent volunteers in the education of our students, and does all this within the limited budget restraints of a private school. We are grateful to the Art Literacy volunteers who dedicate many, many hours to the planning and presentation of our Art Literacy program and who make the Our Lady of Lourdes Art Literacy program a success.

Pizza With the Pastor

Joan Mastell
Principal
St. Agatha School
Columbus, OH

" What a wonderful chance for me to get to know the kids and catch up on all the happenings in the classroom and in the school," said Monsignor David R. Funk, pastor of Saint Agatha Church, as he described his experience with the school's "Pizza with the Pastor" program.

An informal lunch, hosted by Monsignor on the second Tuesday of every month, rewards one student from every class who has exhibited Christian behavior and strong academic effort. Teachers select the sixteen deserving students and a parent letter signed by the principal, is sent home in recognition of the honor. A staff member, chosen by the principal to attend, meets the students at noon for a walk to the rectory for all to enjoy pizza from a local favorite pizza shop, a soda of their choice, and ice cream for dessert.

After prayer, Monsignor begins a typical "Pizza with the Pastor" lunch by having the students introduce themselves, say what grade they are in, and give the name of their teacher. From there, the discussions take off. A recent conversation had both the students and Monsignor in an enthusiastic dialogue about Ohio State's recent football victory over the University of Michigan and the prospects of the local Catholic high school winning their state championship game.

"Pizza with the Pastor" gives both the students and the pastor an opportunity to get to know one another on a more personal level. Monsignor shares his many interests with the students, most often his love of art and history, while they bring their smiles and joys of everyday life to his table.

A trip to the rectory for lunch is not only fun, but educational as well. During the Christmas holidays, Monsignor shares his collection of Christmas ornaments, angels, and statues with the students, often explaining the lives of many saints, or describing the choirs of angels. Frequently, he will talk about his vocation and what it means to serve others. Not long ago, he shared with the students a painting he had received from a parishioner commemorating the First Holy Communion of his grandson.

The staff members enjoy the time with their pastor and with the children. The Director of Religious Education for the parish particularly enjoyed her lunch with the pastor and the students, writing a note to the principal, expressing how much she appreciated talking and laughing with the children. Nearly all school and parish staff members have been invited to this special luncheon. Some have been honored guests on more than one occasion.

"Pizza with the Pastor" is just as meaningful for Monsignor as it is for the students and staff. With a parish of 1,200 families to serve, his schedule does not always allow as much interaction with the students as he would like. These monthly meetings afford him the opportunity to exchange stories with the students and share some common interests. Monsignor is a fan of Shakespeare. A short while ago, he remarked that he had enjoyed the two sixth-grade boys who brought their own enthusiasm of Shakespeare to the lunch.

This program helps to create a special camaraderie between the students and the pastor. Recently, after having lunch with Monsignor, an eighth-grader remarked, "Monsignor was fun to be with. I liked talking to him. It was not as intimidating as if he were in church or school."

Following the lunch, Monsignor often receives thank-you notes which the children write on their own, and which he enjoys reading.

This past month, a second-grade boy wrote a very sweet note. Monsignor referred to this note at our Thanksgiving prayer service.

In the fall of 1999, Monsignor was on a sabbatical for six months. A young deacon was assigned to our parish and was anxious to continue the tradition. Thus, for six months, we had "Dining with the Deacon."

Bill of Writes

Sister Theresa Maugle, SSJ
Principal
Saint Genevieve School
Flourtown, PA

Throughout the process for the Blue Ribbon Schools Program at Saint Genevieve School, the following quote was the hallmark of our task: "Vision without action is merely a dream. Action without vision passes the time. Vision with action can change the future!" With vision as our backdrop, we reviewed practices and established a plan for on-going action to renew curriculum practices.

Saint Genevieve School is a community of learners! Learning is a weaving of awareness, perception, and knowledge of facts with inquiry, experience, discovery, understanding, analysis, evaluation and synthesis of concepts. Saint Genevieve School supports student initiated learning by creating an atmosphere of "academic buzz." Students learn through the modeling of "I messages" and affirmation, which show that the school is a community of learners.

There are two closely related content areas with intertwined practices that play essential roles in the school wide curriculum. Each may be separated and implemented as stand alone, however our strategic plan calls us at Saint Genevieve School to practice both areas in an interrelated fashion. Technology and the writing process are used daily and integrated in all subject areas.

The school implements a "Bill of Writes" which states that every student has the right to understand the writing process. Writing is a particular area of focus and skills are emphasized and developed in all content areas. Benchmarks and standards are used to ensure that the remainder of the curriculum challenges every student. This process consists of the following steps: pre-writing, drafting, conferencing, revising, editing, and publishing. Students use several techniques to enhance their pre-writing skills. They brainstorm ideas by using storyboards, picture writing and mapping. When students have attained the pre-writing skills, they begin to draft their ideas in writing. They understand that sentences function together to produce meaning. Students learn to focus on their topic and develop it to the best of their ability. After drafting, they learn to conference with their teacher and/or peers by discussing possible commendations and recommendations in their writing. The next step in the writing process is vital for students because it enables them to revise their writing piece so it conveys the intended message. They have the opportunity to organize the overall flow of the paper and make revisions to ensure the cohesiveness of their paragraphs. When students begin to edit their papers, they correct their sentence structure, spelling, punctuation, and word usage. Finally, students learn to feel comfortable and share their publications with others. Abbreviated examples of the "Bill of Writes" including the standards and benchmarks of the writing process are writing process standard, the student has the right to understand the writing process. The benchmark for grades K-2 is that children will be exposed to different types of literature. Children will learn the beginning steps of the writing process. Pre-writing, drafting, conferencing, revising, editing and publication benchmarks are further delineated for grades K-2. Similar processes are defined for grades 3-5 and grades 6-8 (the revised publication of "Bill of Writes" is available upon request!).

The Strategic Plan also states that the school place emphasis on technology as one of the primary tools to facilitate communication and give students the necessary skills. Students use technology to enhance the classroom themes, explore a concept, and make connections. Through the correlation between technology and classroom instruction, children learn to be independent users of technology and cooperative learners. Dynamic Learning: TIE (Total Immersion Education) It with Technology is a techno-thematic approach developed at Saint Genevieve School. Through the Dynamic Learning process, students explore a concept in many ways, look at it from different perspectives, make connections, and construct their own meaning. Faculty and students use technology to augment classroom learning, to organize, to visualize with idea maps and simulations, to word process, to research via electronic encyclopedias and the Internet and to express their ideas with presentation applications. Computer programs are chosen for their versatility and age-appropriateness. Inspiration is an application used for planning, organizing and concept mapping. Microsoft Word, MS Works and storybook Weaver are employed for word processing stories, reports, letters and notes. Saint Genevieve School believes that a student has the right to have his/her learning augmented by technology. This standard is supported by a series of benchmarks that are the underpinnings for instruction, rubrics, activities and assessment. A Writer's Checklist, TIE It Together with Technology, A Writing Process/Technology Rubric has been created by the technology coordinator to support the intricate role technology has in the school's writing process (available upon request!).

The success of these programs is built on the thematic approach to learning which affords teachers and students involvement in two or more curricular areas and auxiliary fields such art, library, music, etc. Yearly long-term curriculum goals are thematic in nature and determined monthly. The professional community of Saint Genevieve School is a community of learners who has maintained a high quality educational program. They are dedicated to each child's success and are well versed in incorporating current educational trends, techniques and tools to meet and serve the strengths and needs of every child.

The administration and faculty of Saint Genevieve School believe that we can make a difference in the life of a child and a child can change the world. There is no time like the present for the sake of the future. The greatest act of justice is to educate! We embrace this opportunity to educate the future of our Church and the future of our nation.

Cultural Days

Barbara Migrock
Principal
St. Bernadette School
Silver Spring, MD

In 1997, the St. Bernadette faculty developed *Festival Fridays*, a creative cross-curricular program. This school-wide program gives students a broader understanding of different cultures. In 2001, the faculty changed the name of the program to *Cultural Days*. Currently, the school designates four days throughout the school year to highlight a particular culture and/or country.

Teachers incorporate various cross-curricular activities into their lesson plans (i.e., age-appropriate crafts, songs, dance, games, literature, and folklore). Teachers use a variety of methods to help students understand important cultural heritages. For example, during the 2001 *Greek Cultural Day*, Grade Seven teachers assigned projects that included researching the Greek gods. The assignment included the students dressing in Greek costumes as they orally presented myths associated with each god. To further celebrate the culture, student and parent volunteers prepared samples of Greek foods.

St. Bernadette School celebrated the *Australia Cultural Day* during the summer of 2000 when the Olympics were held in Sydney, Australia. Some activities included students, dressed in red, white and blue, marching around the school field for Opening and Closing Ceremonies. The Kindergarten and Grade One students enjoyed edible gold medallion necklaces as they carried American Flags. The primary grades focused on the famous Outback as well as the indigenous animals of Australia. Art projects that focused on Australia's unique animals complimented the learning experience.

The Cultural Day program at St. Bernadette School has been an outstanding success with the participation of all students and faculty. The program continues to evolve and grow as its cultural focus varies year to year. The St. Bernadette faculty is proud to plant the seeds of global understanding in the fertile minds and hearts of its young students.

St. Hilary School's Enrichment Program

Patricia Nugent
Principal
St. Hilary School
Fairlawn, OH

Begun in 1997, St. Hilary's Enrichment Program grew out of the concerns of parents and educators that students needed to be challenged. Sr. Carol Joy Cincerelli, H.M., who has been director of enrichment at St. Hilary for six years, designed the program. She has been a teacher for more than thirty-seven years in various schools and districts throughout the Diocese of Cleveland. Staffing, budgeting and scheduling are supported by the school administration, and the program is open to all students from kindergarten through eighth grade. The majority of St. Hilary's students are exposed to many cultural opportunities; the Enrichment Program seeks to build upon these experiences and include those who have not had that exposure.

The overall goal of the enrichment program is to teach children to think uniquely and creatively though exposure to classic stories, the visual arts and music. While this method is entertaining, it has been based on research proving that students learn best through the correlation of knowledge and the arts. Each class is developed by using

Bloom's Taxonomy of higher level thinking skills and culminates in a hands-on project.

Content areas feature artists, musicians and writers of fairy tales and classic stories. The visual arts are used in most lessons to affect both right and left brain learning. The philosophy of this program is to challenge all students according to their ability. Students are encouraged to use critical thinking skills while also being challenged to be creative in their work. This carries over into their traditional studies such as religion, language, math and science. Students do not receive grades in enrichment so that they may concentrate on learning for enjoyment rather than achieving the highest grade.

Located in a large classroom near the front entrance to the school, the Enrichment Center takes students into another world from the moment they enter. A timeline of artists, musicians and writers runs along the top of the walls. Prints by famous artists as well as student art work hand throughout the room. While the students work they listen to classical music. Class time is a combination of learning about artistic styles, the artists themselves and their lives, their historical times and their struggles and triumphs. Then the students are encouraged to create their own works of art.

This program is challenging and engaging as well as faith-filled. Students imagine themselves in the mind and spirit of artists such as Van Gogh, and then write an imaginary page from his diary. One of these pages might include his thoughts on, "How can I keep on living when so many have rejected my work?" Students come away from the class not only with knowledge of artists and their contributions, but also with empathy and understanding that sometimes the struggles in one's life can lead to greatness. They study the heavy strokes of paint and swirls of color Van Gogh used in *Starry Night, Sunflowers* and *Vincent's Bedroom.* Students then create their own landscape or bedroom by mixing paint or melting heavy strokes of crayon on paper over a warming tray. Students discuss how each artist has used his or her gifts from God to better our world. Small groups working together allow all students to exchange ideas and cooperate in creating an individual or group project.

The fairy tales of Oscar Wilde are among the favorites of St.

Hilary's primary students and are enriched by large (6' x 9'), hand painted fabric story quits of his books, including *Selfish Giant, The Happy Prince* and *The Star Child*. These quilts motivate the students to want to know more about the man who wrote these wonderful stories. Discussion of Wilde's sons and their love of stories help the students understand Wilde's talent for storytelling, as well as how he wrote the stories to become a part of history. The students illustrate their own booklets of Wilde's fairy tales and keep them as a reminder of his work. They then move on to the tales of Hans Christian Andersen and the Brothers Grimm.

Sixteen story quilts are displayed over the school year as students study the works of that particular person. The Enrichment Center has been compared to a "hands-on museum" which is exactly what it was intended to become. Sister Carol Joy and her students try to recreate the worlds of Leonardo da Vinci, Mary Cassatt, Grant Wood, Claude Monet, Beethoven, Brahms and so many others who have left wonderful works for all to enjoy.

Sister Carol Joy links the community to her work in the Enrichment Program by inviting speakers and parents into her classroom so that they can model creativity at home and elsewhere. She firmly believes that with the pressures and violence confronting young people today, it is important to expose them to the beautiful world of creativity.

Community Service Projects

Ms. Adele Nunez
Cathedral-Carmel School
Lafayette, LA

The Religion Program at Cathedral-Carmel School is fundamentally solid in teaching the Catholic religion to our students through varied learning styles. The program embraces our internal faith-filled community and also provides outreach to our external community. Every student at Cathedral Carmel School is continually provided the opportunity to be touched in the spirit of Jesus Christ throughout their young educational careers.

The school year begins in August with the Opening Mass, which is held in the Cathedral of St, John the Evangelist. Here, we welcome more than 800 students back to the campus. During August, the Campus Ministry team, composed of 54% of the eighth graders, elects officers for the year and organizes planned activities. These team members and the officers serve as role mode ls in the Christian services and activities in which they engage. Services include visiting the De La Salle Christian Brothers Retirement Center, performing a Living Nativity at Christmas festivities, serving as ambassadors during school functions, as well as many other roles as needed throughout the school year. Our eighth grade students participate in a Spiritual Retreat in August to bring them together as the leaders of the school

In September, as part of the religion curriculum, the grade levels select their community service projects. For the 2001-2002 school year the following services have been selected:

PreKindergarten	Placemats for the elderly in the St. John Seniors Program
Kindergarten	Good Deed Beads for our twinned New York School
1st Grade	Cards for the Kairos Inmates (Women's Prison)
	Good Deed Beads for our twinned New York School
2nd Grade	Cards for local nursing home and Kairos Inmates
3rd Grade	Cards for residents of the local Deaf Center
4th Grade	Collecting children's magazines and books for Faith House, a local shelter for abused women and their children.
5th Grade	Bake cookies for Kairos retreat.
6th Grade	Donate new and used children's books for Foster Child Program
	Prepare cookies for Kairos Retreat

7th Grade	Anti-Family Violence Awareness - create posters to display in display in local businesses about Faith House, a home for abused woman and children
	Donate color books and colors for Faith House.
8th Grade	Serve the needy at St. Joseph's Diner, a local diner for the homeless and underprivileged

On October 4th, the feast day of St. Francis of Assisi, the three third grade classes bring their family pets to school for the annual Blessing of the Pets. One of the priests or deacons affiliated with the school offers a special blessing for the pets to remain safe in the upcoming year. Parents, Grandparents, and friends join in the celebration and several classes come to view the blessing.

Grandparents' Day is a wonderful celebration, each year bringing more than 1,000 visitors to campus. A special Mass is offered for our Grandparents followed by a breakfast and concert by the school band. After the concert, the grandparents are invited to visit the classrooms. Since a majority of the grandparents are alumni of the school, the morning resembles an alumni celebration.

The fifth graders host a Pumpkin Carving the day before Halloween. Parents join in the carving of the pumpkins in the cafeteria and celebrate in the students preparing to light the spirit of Jesus in their hearts. At the Pumpkin Prayer Service on Halloween, emphasis is placed upon the spiritual analogy of carving out our imperfections and allowing Christ's light to shine through us.

One of the largest celebrations on campus takes place in November for the All Saints Day Mass in which all the third grade students dress as saints they have studied. This procession and Mass is followed by a reception in the cafeteria for the students and the parents. The Veterans Day Mass is also one of the school's largest celebrations. Members of the local VFW process into Mass along with veterans from the faculty and staff. This year in 2001, Bishop Edward O'Donnell celebrated the Mass and the Cathedral-Carmel Choir was joined by a bagpiper.

In December, Children Helping Children truly represents its name. Students turn in money from chores, allowances, and donation to the school. In turn, the school purchases clothes, gifts, and other necessities for local families identified through the Sisters of Charity and the Sisters of Mt. Carmel. Since 1983, over $27,000 has been distributed to needy children in the community. Also, the school choir, band and Campus Ministry participate in the Festival of Lights, a community celebration of Christmas. Campus Ministry participates as a Living Nativity.

During Catholic Schools Week in January the school alumni, numbering over 7,000, are invited back to campus for a Mass and reception. The school also hosts a dinner for the Teacher of the Year, Distinguished Graduate, and Achiever/Supporter. The Academic Pep Rally honors those students maintaining above average grades.

Late February generally marks the beginning of Lent. Students from second and third grade prepare by participating in the Sacrament of Reconciliation. Students from third through eighth also make the Way of the Cross in St. John's Cathedral.

Early April is Easter, signaling the start of Spring. Second-grade students study and prepare to receive the Sacrament of the Eucharist. These students are prepared for their First Communion by their teachers and several classroom assistants.

The May Crowning celebration at Cathedral Carmel School is a joyous occasion. An eighth-grade girl is selected to crown Mary and is escorted by one of the eighth-grade boys. The crown is presented by a kindergarten girl and boy. All the students bring flowers and line the walkways to the church with their flowers. Inside the Cathedral, students recite the rosary as each decade is lead by a different grade level. Prayer services for the Kindergarten and Eighth Grade students take place in the Cathedral of St. John to signify their advances in their educational careers.

The French Exchange Program was initiated because of the affiliation the school shares with the De La Salle Christian Brothers. Our sister school, St. Joseph's School (in Dijon, France), is also a Christian

Brothers School. The students correspond with one another beginning up to six months before the initial visit. Every other year, the Cathedral Carmel eighth-grade French students visit Dijon for a nine-day exchange study. The following April, the exchange is completed when the Dijon students visit our campus. During their visit, a French Mass is held in honor of our visitors.

Aside from this chronology of monthly events, our Cathedral Carmel students are spiritually renewed through numerous daily prayers, weekly Mass, monthly Benediction, and annual Sacrament of Reconciliation. We are blessed also by having the De La Salle Christian Brothers and the Sisters of Mount Carmel on campus. Their contributions and presence among the children further enrich our Religion Program.

Transitioning Program

Sr. Carolyn Marie Schaffer, SND
Principal
Ladyfield Catholic School
Toledo, OH

At Ladyfield Catholic School we are particularly proud of our transitioning program. The program is many-faceted. It benefits our preschool, kindergarten, and first-grade students, students who transfer to Ladyfield from another school, and our eighth graders as they prepare for high school. It involves assessment, classroom visits, family interviews and evening parent sessions.

Before being admitted to preschool, age-eligible children are screened by an assessment team. Activities conducted at the various stations assess vision, dental, hearing, and speech development, gross and fine motor abilities, visual perception and auditory processing skills. Students who are new to Ladyfield at the kindergarten level are also screened.

To ease the transition to daily classes, the preschoolers are "phased in" during the first four days of school. This 2:7 adult to student ratio allows for highly individual attention to the students to acclimate them to their environment. Kindergarten students are phased in the first two days of school with fourteen students attending each. In May, the class visits the first grade classroom. The children are free to ask questions of the first-grade teacher and her aide. Kindergarten students are also encouraged during the last month of the school year to purchase or pack a lunch to eat in the school cafeteria with one of their parents. They are also measured for the uniforms they will begin to wear the following year.

Transfer students who wish to enter other grades are invited to spend a day at Ladyfield with the class they will join. A Ladyfield student acts as host for the visiting student and the visitor participates fully in all the activities of the day. Teacher assessment of the child's math and reading abilities is also conducted. When the new academic year begins, transfer students in grades 2-8 are assigned a student helper to ease their transition.

Just prior to the new academic year, evening parent sessions are held for the parents of Preschoolers, Kindergartners, and first graders, as well as for parents with a child transferring from another school. At the preschool, kindergarten, and first grade sessions, the parents become familiar with the program and receive suggestions as how best to help their child with the adjustment process. At the new student session, parents learn about curriculum, school policies, and school programs. A question and answer period is also part of all sessions.

Ladyfield's doors are open the day before school begins. Preschool, kindergarten, first grade, and transfer students are specifically invited to visit their classrooms and meet their teachers.

Special effort is made to help eighth grade students who are making a decision about which high school to attend. Class visits are arranged to the area Catholic high schools. Assistance is given to students in completing scholarship applications to these schools and in preparing for the High School Placement Test. Students are also released for individual daylong visits to shadow students at the schools of their choice.

The principal personally interviews all incoming preschool families and any families transferring into Ladyfield. They are also given a tour of Ladyfield during school hours if possible.

We have found transitioning program to be one aspect of Ladyfield that students and parents particularly appreciate.

Effective Partnerships

Lois D. Scrivener
Principal
Holy Name of Jesus School
Indialantic, FL

Holy Name of Jesus School in Indialantic, Florida, earned the U.S. Department of Education's Blue Ribbon School of Excellence Award because of its effective partnerships with parents, students, faculty, staff, administration and the community. By looking at the Holy Name of Jesus School Board Committees you can view the success of these partnerships.

The School Board consists of nine members from the community, and the Home and School President, the principal, the assistant principal, a faculty representative and the pastor. It is effective because it allows the school to tap into the resources and expertise of the community. The Holy Name of Jesus School Board received the NCEA Outstanding School Board Award in 2000. The board committees are where the work of the board is accomplished:

- The Long Range Planning Committee held five stakeholders meetings from May to June 2000 that involved all members of the community, teachers, staff, parents, students, opinion leaders, parishioners and administrators. The responses were collated and the goals and strategies were included in a written long-range plan that was distributed to all school families and members of the parish.

- The Technology Committee oversaw the growth from two computers in the school office to 120 PC's with a state of the art technology lab all connected to the Internet. There are four computers in each classroom along with telephones and direct television. In 1999, the school received the *Today's Catholic Teacher Innovations in Technology Award* seven years after the committee was formed.

- The Facilities Committee supervised the enclosure of the main office building, the construction of covered patios, the renovation of the Science Laboratory, the purchase and installation of ground rubber for the playground and the organization of parent workdays. The committee was instrumental in implementing school supervision of its own custodial personnel, therefore providing a clean and safe environment for the students.

- The Home and School Association consists of all school parents and is represented on the School Board by the Home and School president. Over 11,000 volunteer hours were recorded last year. In recent years, over $70,000 a year has been raised, of which $40,000 goes directly to the school budget. The excess funds are distributed through a Mini-Grant Program. The program allows the faculty and staff to request items for the classrooms. A committee of parents decides which grants should be sent to the principal for approval. Mini-Grant money has been used to purchase keyboards for music, to build two covered patios, to purchase new flooring for the Middle School hallway, to buy maps for Social Studies, to build a butterfly garden, to build the Resource Room and to purchase resources for Special Education services. In 2000, the NCEA Distinguished Parent Partnership Award was presented to Holy Name of Jesus Home and School Association for their development of the Mini-Grant Program.

- The Finance Committee prepares budgets, decides on tuition increases and presents the tuition increase to the parents at a Home and School Association meeting. The Educational Endowment Fund, begun in 1990, reached one million dollars by 2000 and is presently at 1.5 million.

- The Public Relations and Recruitment/Retention Committees work together. Both committees have been successful in the promotion of the school by keeping the Annual Report and the school brochure up-to-date. News and information about Holy Name of Jesus School is published in the school and parish newspapers as well as local newspapers. The retention rate at the school has gone from 48% to 99% over the past seven years and enrollment has grown from 138 to 575.

- The Curriculum Committee is a resource for teachers in deciding on new textbooks, field trips, guest speakers and special events like the science fairs. By bringing together a group of experts in Special Education, goals and strategies for our Resource Program were written and we are better able to meet the needs of learning-disabled students in coordination with the other special services in the community.

- The Student Life Committee helps the Athletic Director coordinate extracurricular activities in which 97% of our students participate. The committee spearheaded the writing of a Student Life handbook that included a problem-solving procedure, student and parent codes of conduct for athletic events and the requirement that all coaches read *Athletics and the Gospel Mission of the Catholic School* before coaching a team.

The success of Holy Name of Jesus School results from its effective partnerships that utilize the talents of all its stakeholders who make a difference in the lives of children.

IDC: Interdisciplinary Curriculum

Sr. Mary Amata Shina, OSF, Principal
Dr. Jean Patrick, Vice-Principal
Written by Carol Stolow
St. Matthias Catholic School
Somerset, NJ

In September 1997, St. Matthias School launched a new and exciting program in the junior high school with approximately 105 students. Fondly referred to as IDC, this interdisciplinary curriculum utilizes the strengths of its faculty members and students. An extra period was created to allow for IDC to meet daily. The curriculum always contains a literature-based unit as well as other relevant topics, such as an in-depth study of the 2000 presidential election.

IDC is made possible through the combined efforts of the five junior department teachers. Among the subjects taught by this group are Language Arts, Religion, Science, Math, and Social Studies. Student groups are divided among four classrooms. Groups consist of four seventh and eighth graders per group. The groups meet once a day for thirty minutes. The two Language Arts teachers are responsible for the literature-based program. One writes the in-class curriculum and the other develops the IDC projects. The other units are distributed among the remaining teachers. Depending on the subject matter of the unit, the respective teacher is responsible for the concept and the other teachers assist in the creation and execution of the assignments and projects.

Students are given rubrics for each project. It explains the objectives, criteria, due date, and other pertinent information. Each teacher assumes responsibility for one of the four classrooms and this teacher floats from one classroom to another to offer assistance. Folders and/or boxes are used to hold works-in-progress so that no work ends up at home with an absent student. At the end of each project, the five teachers evaluate the work. Grades are averaged into that for the principal subject.

The purpose of IDC is to encourage teamwork. Each fall, students are taken to a YMCA camp to participate in activities requiring teamwork. The faculty found that the seventh and eighth graders bonded during that day and wanted to continue this interaction throughout the school year. Groups contain both seventh and eighth graders, both high and low achievers. The projects are designed to challenge critical thinking skills as well as to allow for multiple intelligences.

At first, teachers were quite ambitious and attempted four different units during the school year. As a result, both teachers and students were exhausted. Three units were covered in the second year and proved to be more manageable. This year, we reduced the program to two units, but we began with a five-week introductory unit designed to build the skills necessary for effective teamwork. These activities helped students to identify their own strengths and weaknesses as well as those of their teammates. Teacher-directed lessons helped to sensitize students to the needs of their group-members and to their own responsibilities to that group.

Our literature-based unit is probably the highlight of the year. This unit involves an introduction to drama, the reading of a novel, and a trip to New York City to see a Broadway show. We rotate the seventh-grade edition of *Les Miserables* by Victor Hugo and *Phantom of the*

Opera by Gaston Leroux. Students read the novels in their reading classes. For *Phantom*, we concentrate on its many literary devices, such as foreshadowing, flashback, setting, characterization, inference, mood, and conflict/resolution. In IDC, there is much emphasis on the use and reference to the mask. Students created masks that reflected their own identities. Students also created a gallery of portraits and descriptions of the characters based on the book's description and class discussions. Participants attended a "wine and cheese" party to view the artwork. Our main focus for *Les Miserables* is on the six dominant themes of the book. In addition, a short unit on theater preceded the students' efforts at scriptwriting, costume, setting, prop design, and performance of skits based on the highlights of the book. Students also had to bring in materials of their own choosing to build a model of a French landmark. Prior to our trip, students are introduced to the music and theatrics of the play they are to see.

Our election unit provided an unexpected bonus. In addition to learning about the campaign and electoral process, and following along with events through the newspapers, TV, and the internet, students were encouraged to keep a scrapbook of the election from September through the end of November, 2001. This scrapbook became a valuable memento of this unprecedented, historic election. Students also had to create a candidate. After developing a platform and a party for their candidate, they introduced their candidate to fellow students.

A science-based unit had each group assigned to one of the nine planets. Students had to learn all they could about that planet and then create an alien. Each group had to provide features for their alien that allowed him to adapt to his environment. To do this, they had to consider their planet's temperature, gravity, gas content, and water (or lack of) supply.

While each unit may be based on one particular subject, other subjects and skills are introduced throughout. During *Les Miserables*, the religion teacher talked about the main character's view of God. The social studies teacher introduced the students to an overview of the French Revolution and the student uprisings. Reading comprehension and writing skills are the bases for many units. Students practice and are graded on their oral skills when presenting their projects to the rest of the junior high students. Problem-solving and critical thinking skills are in use throughout the year. Students can try their hand at acting, drawing, planning and building. Research is also an integral part of the program.

In addition to the units mentioned above, students have been able to share their cultures, including the clothing, food, and objects they have brought from home. They are encouraged to learn about other cultures and to read a book about a culture different from their own. Our school marked the millennium with a time-line around the entire second floor which spanned the last thousand years. The Holocaust was covered and compared to other historical events that highlighted human oppression.

IDC is a learning curve for all of us. Each year we add and change things based on our successes and failures as well as on student responses. We think, as a department, that we are on the right track. IDC has proven to be enriching, both for the students as well as the faculty at St. Matthias School.

St. Ann's Blue Ribbon Band Program

Candace Tamposi-Switlyk
Principal

Written by Gary Snyder, Director,
Fine Arts Program & Band Teacher
St. Ann School
West Palm Beach, FL

The St. Ann Band program, founded in August of 1997, has grown from the dream of one principal and one director into an established Blue Ribbon system of many ideals and concepts. The first question to ask yourself is, "How do you begin building a mandatory program, fourth through eighth grade, from scratch...making it acceptable to all, and eventually into a Blue Ribbon program?" The process is one that involves patience, parents, persistence, perseverance, and potential...and having a great director doesn't hurt either! The most important fundamental component making a Blue Ribbon band program, however, is a supportive and dedicated principal. Fortunately, here at St. Ann's we have just that in Principal Candace Tamposi. This program would not be what it is today without her words of encouragement, strength and support as well as a great faculty and parental base.

How do you develop and begin a Blue Ribbon Band Program? First, meeting with all the parents is a great way to start! Answer their questions, attempt to ease their concerns and reassure them that this will be a great experience for all. Also, provide knowledge, support and encouragement to those who have doubts. Be accessible and willing to talk after hours...I mean really talk! Finally, after all the smoke has cleared, speak to the students. Please make sure you expect a gradual acceptance and do not demand their respect...you always have to earn it.. I have learned to accept the difficulties, criticisms and negative responses while savoring the positive thoughts, supportive ways and shining faces.

After a band program has been established, how does it work? Here at St. Ann's, each student (in grades four through eight) take a band or string instrument. Each grade receives ninety minutes of band instruction per week. The fourth and fifth graders have two thirty minute full rehearsals and one thirty-minute small group. What is a small group? A small group is flutes, clarinets and similar instrumental players in one thirty-minute grouping. They are sometimes pulled out of class but it is not required that they do so. Students in grades six through eight receive two forty-five minute rehearsals per week with no small groups. The fourth grade is called the Junior Band, the fifth is the Symphonic and the sixth through eighth is the Wind Ensemble. During each rehearsal, the students warm-up their instruments by plying one of the Circle of Fifth scales and arpeggios. Next, they tune their instruments, identifying by ear if their sound is sharp, flat or in tune. Correction of the non-tuned instrument is taught and the students are expected to know this. Next, a piece of music is rehearsed and analyzed by the ensemble. Finally, at the end of class, either sight-reading and/or questions are answered. During these rehearsals, I play my trumpet or any instrument that is in front of me. I think this helps earn the students respect by "leading by example," and it's also a lot of fun for me as well! I also let the students take turns directing the class. This, I believe, gives them a new "view" of the classroom scene. I finally have a music technology course in which all grades, fifth through eighth, get to write, arrange, perform and even publish, if they can, the song(s) that they have created. It all depends on the desire of the student or group.

For those students who are interested there are before and after school sectionals. They are similar to the fourth and fifth grade small groups: same instruments, but all grades four though eight are welcome. Private lessons are offered after school, as well, one day per week for those interested. Finally, I have formed two Jazz Bands here at St. Ann's and they are the selling point of the program. I highly recommend creating this type of group! The first group is called the Junior Jazz band. This ensemble consists of any fourth grader who is interested in Jazz, but not quite ready for the advanced group. The second of the two groups is the Advanced Jazz Band. This ensemble consists of some fourth graders but mostly fifth through eighth. It has a total of thirty-five players and has become more of a Jazz Orchestra than band. In this group officers are elected by the players. A President, Vice-President, Secretary and Treasurer help oversee procedures and practices. Also, Mr. Floyd, a local guitar and rhythm specialist, comes in and helps the rhythm section during practices.

Now that you have your program established and organized, what do you do with it? At St. Ann's, the band program is shared with the school, church, and the community. The bands perform at many school concerts and functions during the academic year: for example, at events such as Grandparent's Day, Christmas Pageants, Spring Shows, Musicals and Fashion shows, to name only a few. The scientific aspect of band is utilized during Science Fun-Tier Day and the multicultural aspect is brought out during Multicultural Awareness Day. The bands also travel and perform throughout the community as well, with the Jazz band leading the way.

The Jazz Band has performed at several community centers and public venues in which they have been mistaken for a group well past their years. Competitions, festivals and even overseas performances are currently being planned. These players, along with all the other band students, have had the opportunity to view cultural events outside of the school, for example, shows like, "The Zephros Quintet," "Gumbo Jazz," and "MytholoJazz." These shows were performed nationwide and seen by the students at our local venue, the Kravis Center. The Kravis Center is the locus of the Florida Philharmonic and a venue where other great performers display their talents. This leads to an opportunity for St. Ann students to try out for a series by the Kravis Center entitled, "Young Performers - Center Stage." Individuals try out and will hopefully get their chance to shine on the Kravis stage.

The final portion of involvement at St. Ann's is, of course, the religious experience. Any student who is ready may participate in First Friday mass and every Wednesday Prayer Service. During these performances, religion and musical expression become one and all involved benefit from the experience. Special occasions like Christmas Eve Mass and Easter bring the Catholic faith to life. The band program adds to the Blue Ribbon program by building character as well as musical concepts.

With all of these aspects and values in place (foundation of organization, involvement of students, parents, community and religious experience), the need to pursue and expand towards the future is always on the horizon. For example, through Principal Tamposi's efforts, a new building is in the works that, when completed, will provide rooms for a keyboard/music technology lab, guitar studio and, hopefully, a steel-drum ensemble. A pep-band and full orchestra and chamber groups are also in the works.

In conclusion, to answer the question "What makes up a Blue Ribbon Band Program?" I believe a strong administrative position, positive parents and students along with a dedicated and respected director is a good start. However, there is no one definitive recipe, or person, that will produce a great program. It takes a mixture of all that I have described and more to produce a Blue Ribbon Band Program...and here at St. Ann's we're just getting started!

Peer Ministers

Maureen Trenary
Principal

Written by Elaine Nikrad, Assistant Principal
Our Lady of Grace School
S. Edina, MN

O ur school has a long history of being committed to social justice. Several of our education subcommittee meetings were dedicated to discussing the two feet of social justice: the theological framework and social outreach. As we were discussing the "dignity of the human person," we realized how social justice issues always seemed to reach out to those we don't know well, yet the "dignity of the human person" in the person of those closest to us was an equally important issue. It really applies to the students who are sitting right next to you in the classroom, in the lunchroom, and on the bus. We began brainstorming ways that we could help connect the ideas of respect, acceptance, and inclusion to the students in our own community. One of the parents on the committee shared her daughter's high school experience of being a peer minister. As we talked, we became more and more excited about the concept of our eighth graders as leaders who would be advocates for respect, acceptance, and inclusion. Our journey to learn about peer ministry had begun.

The first step was to look at models of successful programs. We looked at bibliographies from the internet, we talked to our guidance counselor, but the materials we received from the neighboring Catholic high school was the most influential. As we read their literature, we were aware that we would need to modify their program from a high school based model to one that would work for a K-8 school. At the same time, it was apparent that this was a program we wanted to pursue.

To get our students as excited as we were, we decided to bring in students from the high school to share their experiences with our seventh graders. Interested seventh graders then filled out an application form to become peer ministers and got two recommendations from faculty. On their applications, students gave reasons for joining such as they "wanted an opportunity to help others" and the program "will give me a chance to interact with younger kids and share ideas."

The training sessions included the areas of communication skills, faith development, and peer mediation skills. There were reflections and discussions about the importance of listening, and then students practiced steps for active listening. A formal step by step process for peer mediation was taught, using the student-workshop skills as outlined in "Mediation Skills" produced by Sunburst Corporation.

Peer ministers were to have a twofold mission: to promote an inclusive, compassionate school community through organized activities and to assist students with typical school-centered growing up problems and act as a listener, an advisor, and mediator for conflicts. As part of our first objective, peer ministers last year sponsored "Say Hi to Everybody Day" on Wednesdays. First teams of ministers went into each class and talked about the importance of greeting. They role-played good examples and poor examples of greeting one another and then left posters which reminded students about eye contact, a smiling face, and friendly tone of voice. We also are developing a New Students' Club. This year each peer minister received the name and address of a new student and sent them a welcoming letter late in the summer. There was a gathering celebration the first week of school which included a scavenger hunt to help the new students become familiar with the building. We will use feedback from our new students and our current eighth-grade peer ministers to keep developing and improving this program. Another effort to build a compassionate environment is our "Prayer Box," located in the library. Students may leave their intentions in this box and every month peer ministers will pray a decade of the Rosary for those intentions.

Our peer ministers have also been used to provide peer mediation. They use their training to apply a step by step process to define the problem, brainstorm solutions, and then write an agreement acceptable to both parties. They clearly set and enforce the ground rules of no "put downs" and no interrupting. Although this is not a solution to all conflict, it does provide a channel for students to work out minor problems and it gives both the mediators and the disputants a chance to work cooperatively toward a resolution to a conflict. Taylor, a third grader student said, "They listened, asked questions, and then helped us come to an agreement."

Peer ministry provides our eighth graders with an opportunity to develop leadership skills. Their commitment to work toward building a more compassionate, caring school community is a chance to put their faith into action.

A School Behavior Plan

Elizabeth Trenkamp
Principal
St. Pius X Elementary School
Edgewood, KY

I believe the one program that has made a significant impact on the entire school program would be our Behavior Plan. Five years ago we had a discipline plan that was very negative. Students had demerit cards that were marked whenever they were not in compliance with any school rule. After five marks on this card students had detention to serve that week. After several detentions, out of school suspension was given. Several issues made us rethink the program.

First, the children could get a demerit for not having a nametag or for hitting someone. This seemed to be very odd that the weight of these two things would be the same. Second, there were usually 15-30 students per week in detention and several suspensions each week. Third, the atmosphere of the school was very negative and students were fearful a lot of the time. Fourth, out-of-school suspension provided a free day for breaking the rules.

In order to change the environment of the school, increase the morale of the teachers and students, and help guide students to take responsibility for their own actions, we implemented the following. First, we changed the name to Behavior Plan because the word "discipline" has a negative connotation. Second, we changed the demerit cards to Incentive Cards. Instead of highlighting negative behavior, we began acknowledging what the students are doing right. There are 45 spots on the incentive cards for teachers to sign. When a card is full, the student can exchange it or save it for a reward. Incentives can be given for a variety of reasons such as, being in dress code, being prepared for class, including homework), returning signed slips on time, being quiet in balls, restrooms, and during announcements, Christian behavior, and other reasons designated by the teacher. Incentive rewards are as follows:

One Card: Principal's Treasure Box or Candy;

Two Cards: Coupon book for 1 coke, 1 candy bar, 1 extra dessert at lunch, 1 treasure box gift or fifteen minutes extra recess time at lunch with a buddy (2 cards each);

Three Cards: Out of Uniform Day or Ice Cream Sundaes (December and May);

Four Cards: Teacher helper for a day or Gift Certificate ($10 Media Play or Toys R Us);

Five Cards: Lunch out with the principal or a field trip.

When a student does have a need for correction there are three solutions. One is "Think Sheets." They are used to help the student reflect on the situation. They come to the Principal or Assistant Principal to discuss three questions: what were you doing?, What should you be doing?, and How are you going to fix the problem? This gives the children an opportunity to think about what they have done and take responsibility for their own actions. Think Sheets are then signed by the teacher, principal, student, and sent home for parent signature (copy enclosed). The second way is Conduct Referrals. These deal with repeated misbehavior or more severe incidents. A student is issued a Conduct Referral by the teacher and is then assigned detention for that week. The third way is In School Suspensions. They are reserved for much more serious and/or chronic problems.

As a result of these changes, the children are much happier and less fearful about being in school Teachers know they are getting support from both the administration and the parents. There are many weeks we have no detentions, and when we do there are far fewer students who need to stay. All in all it has really boosted morale throughout the school and is teaching children about being responsible for their own behaviors. Our first goal as educators should be to guide children to become responsible adults. We believe our plan will help us achieve this goal while providing a pleasant and positive atmosphere conducive to quality teaching and learning. It also incorporates our desire to foster a Christian atmosphere where every student, teacher and parent respects one another.

Practices of Blue Ribbon Catholic Schools, 2001

ST. PIUS X SCHOOL
THINK SHEET

1. Take sheet to Miss Trenkamp or Mrs. Raker for discussion.
2. Grades 1-3 we will help you record your answers.
   Grades 4-8 answer questions completely and in sentences.
3. Sign the sheet.
4. Have teacher sign the sheet.
5. Return to Miss Trenkamp or Mrs. Raker with the sheet.

Name_____Grade_____Homeroom_____
Teacher_____Date_____TIME_____

A. What were you doing?

B. What should you be doing?

C. How are you going to fix the problem?

Student Signature_____
Teacher Signature_____
Principal Signature_____TIME_____

6. Take this Think Sheet home and discuss the situation with your parents. After this discussion, have your parents fill out and sign the bottom section. You should return this sheet tomorrow to Miss Trenkamp or Mrs. Raker.

A. _____ I have reviewed and discussion this situation with my child.

B. _____ The following comments are the result of our discussion.

Parent Signature_____

Reading Resources

Marilyn S. Valatka
Principal

Mrs. Patricia Kobyra
Curriculum Supervisor
St. Timothy School
Chantilly VA

St. Timothy School has successfully combined the attributes of a 'good' school and an 'effective' school. St. Timothy School has an atmosphere of caring and support that extends to each individual student. Although caring and support are not directly measurable, the actions that express those sentiments are measurable. The faculty and staff are encouraged and given the tools to identify and meet the individual needs of each student whether those needs involve enrichment or support. A fully staffed and full-time learning Center with two Learning Disability teachers and a Reading Specialist and a Resource teacher assists the teaching staff with individual student concerns. Their response and coordination with the classroom teacher are as varied as the needs of the students.

Referral for services involves a multi-step process. First, either a parent or teacher may refer a student to the Center by completing a referral form. This form is given to the Learning Center Screening

Committee that is comprised of the Principal, the Curriculum Supervisor, the Learning Center teachers, the Reading teacher and the Speech/language teacher. Using a packet of written information such as classroom tests, standardized tests, examples of written expression, reading evaluation, previous report cards, and teacher narratives, the teacher and/or parent presents the student to the Screening Committee and advocates for the child. They discuss their concerns and provide information that supports student referral. Especially important is a discussion of what has already been done to assist the student. Upon evaluating the information presented, the Committee will make its recommendation. The recommendation may include speech/language screening, additional reading evaluation, or a referral for ADD/ADHD evaluation, and finally a referral for a four-core evaluation to determine special education needs.

Never lost in the process is the desire of the entire St. Timothy professional community for each and every child inside the building to succeed academically. The goal is to provide a learning opportunity for students that will ensure that not only will they learn, but also they will develop a love of learning. Children who are struggling academically become easily frustrated. The St. Timothy School teaching team, from the classroom teacher to the principal, tries to identify children with potential learning problems very early in their school career so frustration never becomes a problem.

The learning Center advocates for the parent and the student by presenting the necessary documents to the local public school screening committee. One of the Center's teachers attends all screening, eligibility, and, if applicable, IEP meetings. It is the responsibility of the learning Center to implement the IEP document of the student attending St. Timothy School. The St. Timothy Learning Center provides the opportunity for a 504 Plan to be implemented for those students who qualify for classroom accommodations. The school's Resource teacher is the manager of the 504 Plan documents and over sees its implementation within the regular classroom. The 504 Plan is written by the classroom teacher, the parents and the principal designee. Other educators involved in the student's academic career may also be included in the process. Included within the Learning Center is a speech/language pathologist who provides individual screening and remediation for those students who may be in need of services.

The Reading lab is a key component to meeting the academic needs of special needs students as well as all students at St. Timothy School. It serves the entire school community and provides a reading screening of all students new to the school. The screening consists of both a decoding and reading comprehension evaluation. Both formal and informal evaluations of students suspected of having a reading deficit are provided. The Reading lab is equipped with the latest in computer technology and software and the Kurzweil Reading system that utilizes a multi-sensory approach to enhance the learning of the reading disabled student. The system provides assistance for all students who may benefit from being able to use both visual and auditory skills in the reading process. The St. Timothy Learning Center, in existence since 1984, has been a shining example of the principal's goal of ensuring that all students will be able to receive a Christian education.

St. Timothy School has a complete complement of full-time "special" teachers, including Art, Music, Computer, library, Health and PE. These teachers work closely with each other and the classroom teachers to enrich and support the basic curriculum.

The Principal at Saint Timothy School both thinks and acts "outside the box" so to speak. Mrs. Valatka is excellent at assessing the gifts of her teachers and the needs of the students. She makes both staff decisions and program decisions that may not be typical, but clearly are a creative and effective response. A few years ago, it was determined that the needs of the school community would be best met by the creation of a new position-a Curriculum Supervisor. In a school as large as St. Timothy School, frequently an Assistant Principal serves to assist in administrative and discipline issues. The principal determined that a greater need rested in the smooth implementation of curriculum and support of school staff. As a result, the focus of the Curriculum Supervisor includes the learning needs of the students, the support, training and evaluation of the staff, the implementation of the curriculum and the evaluation of resources. The Curriculum Supervisor works closely with the principal, the faculty, and the Learning Center to address the needs of the students. She coordinates and sometimes provides in-service opportunities for staff. In general, her main goal is to serve as a resource and sounding board so that staff members may do the best possible job for the students. Mrs. Valatka has a wonderful rapport with her staff as well as the parents of the Saint Timothy School Community. This fosters the communication vital to being both a 'good' and an 'effective' school.

Parental support and involvement are significant factors in becoming and maintaining the status of a Blue Ribbon School. St. Timothy has a very active PTO, a START (Saint Timothy Awareness Round Table—a program that address drug and alcohol problems) committee and a generous group of volunteers whose presence in the school is welcomed with open arms.

Ultimately, it is not one of these things, but the smooth combination and interwoven nature of all that contributes to Saint Timothy School being A National Blue Ribbon School of Excellence.

A Winning Combination: Parental Involvement and Character Counts

Anita J. Westerhaus
Principal
Sacred Heart School
West Des Moines, IA

What enabled Sacred Heart School, West Des Moines, Iowa, to win recognition as a 2001 USDE Blue Ribbon School in our first attempt? Of the many programs we could cite, the difference was surely our emphasis on "shared leadership." This characteristic is best evidenced in two ways: both through daily parental involvement and through the longer-term process we followed to implement our character education program, "Character Counts."

While some schools may shy away from too much parental involvement, Sacred Heart has made it a point of emphasis for more than twenty years. We embrace shared leadership in everything we do. The result is that faculty and staff are committed to excellence because the parish and parents are dedicated partners. "Constant Caring, Learning, Growing" has become our school motto. Our focus on a strong sense of community, together with excellent educational opportunities and achievement, has fueled phenomenal growth at Sacred Heart. Visitors, particularly parents of potential students, consistently report an impression of having visited a special place.

At Sacred Heart, we believe our mission is to assist parents in the Catholic education of their children by building on Christian ideals and attitudes established at home and by working toward development of true Christians who affirm the diversity that exists in our world. Recognizing that parents are the primary educators of their students and partners with the school in their education, Sacred Heart School has developed an exemplary parent volunteer program. More than 85% of all Sacred Heart parents volunteer time in some capacity to support the school.

Wide participation by parents, as well as volunteers from the general parish community, speaks to the reach of the school's caring community and to the desire on the part of Sacred Heart School staff to leverage all available resources to provide the richest learning and spiritual experience possible for students. Parent volunteers help with school security by directing traffic and managing the Visitor's Desk in the school lobby. Volunteers assist in the classrooms, the library, the lunchroom, and on the playgrounds. Parents help make copies and coach athletic teams. And parents regularly partner with teachers to provide the inspiration and impetus for experimenting with new programs as they identify unique needs and seek solutions to meet them. Parents serve on a variety of established and ad hoc committees, including the Parish Board of Education, School Improvement Advisory Committee, Home and School Association, and the Technology 21 Committee.

Pervading all Sacred Heart School activities is the ongoing focus on building and nurturing community, and a focal point of that effort is our own, unique application of the "Character Counts" program. Nationally, the program teaches six pillars of character: trustworthiness, respect, responsibility, fairness, caring, and citizenship. At Sacred Heart, we've added a seventh pillar — faith — the foundation for all character and the source of strength.

Through Character Counts, students learn to recognize appropriate behaviors and actions that help make the world a better place. These in turn provide the students with good moral guideposts. The program challenges students to find their own examples of "good character" among their classmates, and it inspires students to take the initiative in choosing their own behaviors. Character Counts is bearing fruit as we hoped when we first adopted it. Students are noticeably kinder to each other and have shown more respect for each other and staff members.

Again, it was our emphasis on Shared Leadership and trying to promote a healthy peer climate that resulted in making Character Counts part of the curriculum in 1998. After parents noticed poor sportsmanship at athletic events and provided feedback to school staff that the students did not seem to be consistently demonstrating behaviors that Sacred Heart School stood for, teachers and parents together began to research possible solutions. This grassroots effort ultimately uncovered the Character Counts program that we introduced.

Staff members read extensively about several programs, visited other schools with various programs in place, and, with administration approval, proposed the program to the rest of the staff and the parish Board of Education. Unlike top-down, mandated changes, this grassroots effort resulted in a well-received program in which teachers and staff have a real sense of ownership. With the approval of the administration, staff and Board, the Character Counts program was added to the curriculum, and training sessions were held for the parents to ensure they understood the intent and content of the program so that it could be reinforced at home.

The addition of the Character Counts program as a standard part of the curriculum has made it easier to teach students about proper Christian behavior. The program brings home in a concrete way the teachings of Christ to the students. It aligns perfectly with the tenets of faith taught at Sacred Heart. Each member of the Sacred Heart community is challenged to not only talk about, but also to model proper behavior.

Leadership first by Sacred Heart eighth grade students in following the pillars of Character Counts encouraged their ownership of the program and the subsequent acceptance of the program by younger students. The activities associated with the program, and ongoing reinforcement of positive behavior, has gained universal acceptance in the school. A monthly Gospel-infused assembly is held to recognize students who have been nominated by their classmates as excellent models of one of the pillars. While it is an honor to be nominated, students know it is also an honor for the student who made the winning nomination, because he or she was best able to identify and articulate a good role model for the pillar.

In summary, of the Sacred Heart programs cited by the evaluator following our Blue Ribbon Site Visit, the combination of shared leadership and Character Counts were foremost. Making EVERYONE associated with the school — students, parents, administration, faculty, staff and the parish as a whole — responsible for achieving our shared vision, has truly been the "secret" to our success.

Student Mission Statements

Jackie Zufall
Principal
St. Paul School
North Canton, OH

"St. Paul School ignites enthusiasm, inspires excellence and nurtures life-long learners in our Catholic Community"

As our school mission statement declares, staff, parents, students and community members share a strong vision for educational excellence at Saint Paul School.

Our journey to forming a school mission statement began in 1999. In preparation, staff members read and discussed books related to forming mission statements. We began with Steven Covey's *The Seven Habits of Highly Effective People*. This thought-provoking book gave us an introduction to the mission statement process and helped to educate us about the importance of missions, visions and how they can become lifelong tools. Two books by Laurie Beth Jones, *Jesus, CEO* and *The Path*, gave us a more spiritual look into mission statements as a way of life. Some teachers read entire books, while many read sections of the books to share in small groups.

The school staff and representatives for the students, parish and community, worked with a professional consultant for the school mission statement process. Through our recently completed school accreditation process, we had spent many hours in self-searching activities, identifying our strengths and weaknesses. Now, in preparation for mission statements, we asked ourselves "What is our purpose as a school?" and "What are our priorities?" We discussed "What direction do we want to go?" and "What do we want our school to look like?" All interested parties took part in the process: teachers, principal, priests, representative parents, students and community members. We worked both in groups and individually. We talked excitedly over breakfast and lunch. Through introspection and brainstorming, discussion and consensus a school mission statement was created!

In addition to having a school mission, each member of our teaching staff has developed a personal or professional mission statement. Each mission is a working document which guides us daily as we lead our students on their own educational journey. Using a process similar to the one used to create our school mission, teachers created their own personal and professional mission statements. During the process, drafts were created and then refined with further discussion or personal searching.

Each child at Saint Paul School possesses a personal or educational mission statement. As a staff and community, we strongly believe in the importance of recognizing each student as an individual learner. A personal mission statement allows individual learners to express and celebrate themselves through their own style. During the 2000 - 2001 school year, the staff prepared to lead each of our 440 students as they created their personal mission statements. This part of the process was more challenging. Teachers approached students by considering their specific needs and abilities. For example, kindergarten students who cannot write sentences cannot be expected to understand and convey a personal or educational mission.

As always, teachers had to ask themselves what their students were capable of writing, thinking and doing. What kind of springboard could teachers use to prompt students to embrace the idea of mission statements? How could the idea of mission statements be incorporated in the primary grades? Through some trial and error, each grade level teacher began to discover creative mission-writing approaches to which students could relate.

How do we approach mission statements with students? In Kindergarten the teacher leads simple class discovery discussions focusing on good habits, for example, treating others respectfully, working hard in school, and cleanliness and helping others. These simple "missions" are incorporated in beginning day activities. In first grade, a discussion lead by the teacher prompts students to offer similar "missions" which are written down on medallions or necklaces. Each day upon arrival at school, students choose a medallion or necklace to wear. This helps them to concentrate on a daily mission such as to "Be a friend," "Smile," or "Help someone." Intermediate grade students participate fully in forming individual mission statements. Some teachers use trade books to inspire students. One teacher uses her family genealogy unit to prompt students to look for positive character assets of ancestors or relatives. Another teacher arranges for each fourth grade student to invite a mentor to school. Together they discuss positive character traits, then brainstorm those qualities the child wants to model. Our professional consultant takes the lead with students in grades six, seven, and eight. She uses self-discovery and brainstorming exercises to help them focus on themselves and a personal mission.

A mission statement is only effective if used frequently. To that end, students, teachers, and parents have used a variety of ideas to help students focus on their mission statements and to use them daily as a vision for their lives. Our school mission statement has been reproduced as a colorful poster and is displayed in frames throughout the school. It is an integral part of our correspondence through newsletters, on stationery and on our computer generated report card. It is on our school web site.

Teachers display their missions in professional portfolios, as framed pictures on their desks and as hangings on the classroom wall. They display them on their web pages, in their lesson plans and on bulletin boards. Some examples of teacher missions: "*I seek to honor God in a positive atmosphere of discovery learning while fostering cooperation and respect*" and "*My mission is to nurture, inspire and share with my students, the integrity, honesty and the sometimes uncommon courage, of those who have humbly come before them."*

Through our computer lab, students have the opportunity to type their mission, add graphics and pictures and then display them on classroom walls, on lockers or in the halls. Some classes have made their mission statements into bookmarks. Others have typed them and placed them on the corner of their desks as a daily reminder. Examples of student missions: *"I am the moon glowing love around the world. I am the rain, raining peacefulness"* (3rd grade); *To be the best person I can be. Be a true friend and make my family proud"* (4th grade); and *"...to live life to its fullest so that if I die tomorrow, I can live my life today the way I want to be remembered: a loving person who always remembers the little things in life"* (7th grade).

Teachers use every opportunity to keep student mission statements active. Some include reflection time when they pray at the beginning of every day. This helps students focus daily on their mission. During Catholic Schools Week we started each day with a prayer service designed to reflect our recent parish mission. Of course, our mission statements were a central focus! In fourth grade, a talented parent was invited to work with students to create a mission song that our entire student body loves to sing at mass or assemblies. A sample of the lyrics:

First you must state your mission
Make a list of your dreams and your goals
Then reach out to God's guiding hand
And hold on as the mission unfolds
—Written by Dr. Ben McCabe and Students of Grade 4

Future goals include planning for daily reflection time and developing activities that will keep our mission statements important in our daily lives. We want to discover ways to celebrate the individual learner and to encourage our students to use their mission statements to bring reality to their dreams. And we will follow our mission song:

Learning, loving and laughing
Letting God's light shine in me
Walking with my God day by day
Will help me be the best that I can be.